LONNY
Love

Gloria Lichtenberg

The opinions expressed in this manuscript are solely the opinions of the author and do not represent the opinions or thoughts of the publisher. The author has represented and warranted full ownership and/or legal right to publish all the materials in this book.

Lonny Love
All Rights Reserved.
Copyright © 2015 Gloria Lichtenberg
v3.0

Cover Photo © 2015 Gloria Lichtenberg. All rights reserved - used with permission.

This book may not be reproduced, transmitted, or stored in whole or in part by any means, including graphic, electronic, or mechanical without the express written consent of the publisher except in the case of brief quotations embodied in critical articles and reviews.

Matalon Publishing

ISBN: 978-0-578-15461-9

PRINTED IN THE UNITED STATES OF AMERICA

TABLE OF CONTENTS

1	JANUARY, 1961	1
2	LONNY'S EARLY YEARS	5
3	UP AND DOWN THE RIVERDALE HILL	12
4	LONNY THE ACTOR	15
5	LONNY'S FRIEND WILLIE	19
6	LONNY'S FRIEND KERA	23
7	LONNY THE DRUG DEALER	27
8	LONNY THE DRUG ADDICT	32
9	LONNY'S LOVES	35
10	HIGH HOPES	38
11	A LETTER FROM RICHARD	42
12	SINKING LOWER	45
13	A LETTER FROM LONNY – 1991	48
14	RIKER'S ISLAND	51
15	LONNY'S HEALTH ISSUES	53
16	A LETTER FROM LONNY-1993	57
17	THE BIG DAY ARRIVES - 1994	61
18	MORE LETTERS – 1996	65
19	LIFE ON EAST SEVENTY-FIRST STREET	70
20	FLORIDA, WE'RE HERE!	75

21	MOVING ON, MOVING IN	80
22	SETTLING IN	84
23	SETTLED IN	87
24	LOLA AND THE NOT SO FRIENDLY SKIES	93
25	BANKRUPTCY	96
26	T.V. OR NOT T.V.	99
27	FRIENDS TO THE END	104
28	AN INTERVIEW WITH GREG	106
29	POT LUCK	113
30	PARTY TIMES	118
31	THE END IS NEAR	122
32	HOSPICE	128
33	A FACEBOOK CHAT	130
34	THE FUNERAL	136
35	MATT'S EULOGY	138
36	THE BURIAL	142
37	CLEAN-UP TIME	144
38	CONDOLENCES	147
39	THE UNVEILING	149
40	THE MEMORIES	152
ACKNOWLEDGEMENT AND THANK YOU		155
ABOUT THE AUTHOR		157

JANUARY, 1961

I was five months pregnant with Lonny. It was about 1 PM and Alan, 6, had just come home from school and left the door unlocked. I gave him his lunch, and totally engrossed, he sat eating and watching television. Matt, 3, was playing in his room. I was in the bathroom putting my make-up on and getting ready to go out with them. Suddenly, there was a hand on my mouth and a strange face in the mirror. He was wearing a camel's hair overcoat, probably on his way to work.

He started dragging me into the bedroom. Matt came out to see what was happening, and the man pushed him back into his room and slammed the door.

Still wearing his coat, he threw me on the bed and

got on top of me. I thought to myself, "This is it. I AM GOING TO DIE. It's the end of me and my baby."

I begged him, "Please don't do this to me. I'm pregnant."

He thought for a minute, and then he said, "You're pregnant? Do you believe in God?"

"Yes, I believe in God," I whispered helplessly.

"Turn your head. I'm leaving, but if you call the police, I will come back and kill you," he threatened and dashed out. Alan saw him leaving and asked, "Who are you?" He answered hurriedly leaving the apartment, "Nobody". This "nobody" traumatized me so greatly that I was left with fears that affect me to this day.

I was lucky, because he must have suffered from premature ejaculation, and he had not penetrated me. The front of my dress was soaked with semen. I lay still for awhile until I was ready to face what happened. Still in shock, the first thing I did was call my mother, and then my husband at work and then the housing police. I changed my clothes and stuffed the dress down the incinerator. I later learned that the neighbors had heard their doorknobs rattling. My door had been left unlocked.

It has taken me a long time to get over this experience. Actually, I don't think I ever will. It was then that I understood how it feels when you think that your life is coming to an end. You really believe that, "This is it. I'm going to die."

I know that Lonny has had that feeling in his lifetime many times.

Baby Lonny was a love!

LONNY'S EARLY YEARS

Lon Ian Lichtenberg was born in The Bronx on May 22, 1961. He weighed six pounds and two ounces, was blue-eyed and beautiful. It was a very normal birth, but not so his life to come.

After Lonny was born, I started teaching in public school. I had to get my Master's Degree and take in-service education courses. We had help from my mother, who lived nearby, and a nanny who was there when she was needed. When Lonny was five years old, we decided to send him to a Hebrew School with a full day program. According to school reports he had excellents in every subject. He was doing so well, that the school decided to put him a year ahead. In his case, it was a big mistake. When he moved on to public school, his classmates were older, as were his friends. Unfortunately, even at that early age his choice of friends caused problems!

When he was little, Lonny used to like to swing on a chain that surrounded our house. One day he was swinging and he fell off the chain right on his face. We rushed him to the hospital. Though there was no serious damage to his head, it was very swollen and his eyes were tiny slits. He looked like E.T. and he was in terrible pain. A week later he was swinging on the same chain again. Lesson learned: If at first you don't succeed in breaking your head, try, try again.

As his brothers before him, Lonny was ready to join Little League. When I signed him up, I volunteered my husband to be manager of the team. For some reason, the little players are happy to have their father in charge. They think they have an edge. In this case it did not make a difference because my husband, Frank, was very fair-minded. Lonny hit well and caught well enough, but he did not aspire for the big leagues. He received his trophy, and a picture of him in his uniform appeared in one of the local newspapers.

We were once invited to a friend's house on the Fourth of July. Lonny's friend's father was in the State

Guard. He happened to have a live hand grenade, and he thought it would be a fun experience for the boys if he set it off, all in the spirit of the holiday. It was a successful detonation, but the noise left Lonny slightly deaf for the rest of his life.

When Lonny was nine years old, we were living in a very large development in the eastern part of the Bronx. That is where he had his first "brush with the law." He had surrounded himself with a group of more aggressive peers, the leader of which did a very foolish thing. He had threatened a little girl with a knife, and the girl's mother reported the incident to the police. The "gang", six little hoodlums, including Lonny, was picked up and taken to the local police station. I was called in and asked to answer some questions, some of them personal. The following dialog stands out in my mind from that unforgettable experience:

Police Officer: Mrs. Lichtenberg, what is your date of birth?

Reluctant Me: April 23, 1930.

Indignant Lonny: (After deep reflection) MOM! You lied to me! You said you were twenty-nine!

The seriousness of the situation he was in did not bother him. What deeply disturbed him was that I was really forty years old, and I had deceived him. But he made up for it in his own deceptions in the years to come.

When Lonny entered public school he followed in the shadows of his brothers, Alan and Matt. They were excellent students, well-behaved and liked by their teachers. His achievement was average and his grades soon began to decline. He was small in stature, and in his class photos, he would be seated in front on the floor. In middle school he had trouble academically and with behavior. He was not paving a positive path to high school.

According to Jewish law, when a Jewish boy reaches thirteen years old he becomes a Bar Mitzvah. This means that he is accountable for his actions in life. The services are held in the temple, usually followed by an elaborate catered party.

At the temple, Lonny did the required part of the service that he had memorized, the reading of the Torah, and gave the obligatory speech that sometimes starts out with, "Today I am a man!" We were surprised and proud that he gave an outstanding performance which should have prepared us for his short-lived success as an actor later on, both on stage and in real life.

One year old Lonny
and I chilling out in the Catskills.

Three year old Lonny sang "Hello Dolly"
to a standing-room-only audience.

Five year old Lonny is celebrating his fifth birthday. Alan and I are blowing out the candles.

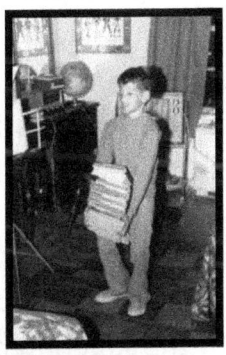

Ten year old Lonny was heavily into books!

UP AND DOWN THE RIVERDALE HILL

When Lonny was thirteen, we moved to a high-rise building in Riverdale, an upscale part of the Bronx. He enrolled in high school located at the bottom of the Riverdale hill. The building we were living in was on the top of the hill. Lonny was even higher when he was introduced to marijuana by our neighbors, for whom he was baby-sitting. This we found out many years later.

The building that we lived in had doormen, and was well looked after by the superintendent, Mr. Gomez, who ran a tight building. We lived on the third floor. Lonny, in his spare time in which he should have spent studying, would stand at his window which looked down on to the parking lot, and would throw down balloons filled with water. One day, as luck would have it, Mr. Gomez walked out of the door and became the perfect target. It could not have been worse if an A Bomb had exploded. He rang my bell, in person, to let me know about the unfortunate incident. Lonny apologized, but he was not really regretful. It was a funny story he could recount to his friends.

It seemed, thereafter, that building services slowed down for us. However, things improved after we made up for the mishap with an abundant Christmas gift.

Lonny always had deep respect for me. He never used a curse word in front of me in his whole life. He once brought a friend for dinner. During the course of our conversation, his friend used an expletive. Lonny was appalled, and he asked the young man to apologize. Through the course of his difficult life, his love and respect for me never waned.

Lonny's brothers, Alan and Matt, were very good students, but Lonny never distinguished himself academically. I was a working mom and did not give him the attention he probably needed. High School was really a problem. Unbeknownst to us, he was already experimenting with some form of drugs. With help and a little bit of luck, he got his diploma and was ready to face the world!

Lonny went to live on his own when Matt decided to move to California. He took over Matt's apartment on Twelfth Street. Surprisingly, he had good taste and furnished his apartment attractively with antique style furniture.

He very much enjoyed company, had many friends and a beautiful Persian cat. He got along well with his neighbors, and the landlord was paid his rent on time. Then things changed.

Lonny had a few jobs, but they didn't last too long. One of my good friends owned a men's clothing store in Manhattan. He hired Lonny, but he only worked for him for about a year. His days of working at a traditional job were over for the time being.

LONNY THE ACTOR

On June 27, 1982, Lonny's picture appeared on the front page of the The Guide, the Entertainment Section of the Sunday Times, which to this day hangs prominently as a poster on our wall. We were so thrilled and so proud. The Times cover showed a picture of him as he appeared at the Actors' Playhouse in an Off-Broadway show called "Broken Toys." He played Randy, a clown, and he sang, danced and played the kazoo, much to our surprise and entertainment. As a talent "maven" and amateur theater critic, I was very impressed and gave him an A rating.

When asked for his background for the playbill, Lonny told them the following:

"I worked with several amateur acting groups which performed wherever they could find free or cheap space. We once performed in a mall, and my mom did the spotlight. The first time I faced an audience I was three years old, and I sang "Hello Dolly" to a standing room only crowd. I got a standing ovation. I took trumpet lessons, so, of course, I can play the kazoo. I know that I can sing falsetto because I have been practicing in the shower."

Some of what he said is actually true. We were staying at a bungalow colony in the Catskills and he sang "Hello Dolly" in front of an audience when he was three years old. Sadly, I wasn't there, so I missed his debut. And yes, he played the trumpet in school. However, I never did hear him sing falsetto in the shower, but it was faultless in his performance.

In order to be a cast member, Lonny had to join Actors' Equity. Imagine, Lonny was a card carrying member of a respected union! Eventually, he had to ask to be suspended.

As of now, he was going on to bigger and better things, or so he thought.....

Randy the Clown in "Broken Toys"
He danced, played the kazoo,
and sang falsetto.
What a talent!

Photo by Carol Rosegg.

On the street where "Broken Toys" played.

LONNY'S FRIEND WILLIE

Lonny was very likeable, fun-loving and giving. In return, throughout his life, he was blessed with wonderful friends.

Willie was one of them. He was Australian, a chef and he was gay. He was also an alcoholic. On several occasions he cooked delicious dinners for us at Lonny's apartment in the East Village. His lamb chops were memorable. We became friendly and kept in touch through the years.

Willie was getting married and he asked me to be a witness at his wedding. It was summer and I was on vacation, so I happily agreed. I was to meet the wedding party at the Marriage Bureau in City Hall.

It was a lovely summer day. As I walked toward City

Hall, I was stopped by a young couple. They asked me if I knew where the Marriage Bureau was. I told them I wasn't sure, but we could try to find it together. We chatted as we walked.

Tom and Susan were from a small town near Syracuse, New York, and decided they wanted to get married in New York City. I told them that I was here for my son's friends' wedding, and that I had been asked to be a witness. They were not aware that a witness was necessary and asked if I would be theirs as well. I happily agreed. Two for the price of one!

We found the marriage courtroom. There were only two other couples waiting, and Tom, Susan and I sat down together. Some of Willie's party began arriving. The three of us watched as they entered the courtroom, astonished by their attire. Some were dressed for a reception at Leonard's, and some were dressed outlandishly and ostentatiously. Tom and Susan looked at me quizzically, as I sheepishly waved at my son, who was dressed in normal attire. I only knew one other person, Kera, about whom I will write later.

All eyes turned to the door as the bride and bridegroom entered. Katie, the bride, was wearing a white wedding gown and a veil, and Willie, the groom, was wearing a tuxedo. Their friends responded audibly to their arrival in the quiet courtroom. The bride and groom joined the rest of the wedding party and awaited their turn, conspicuous by their presence.

Tom and Susan were called, and we entered the chapel together. There was a short ceremony to which I was the witness. When we left we embraced, we exchanged addresses and promised to stay in touch. The event was memorable, in a small way.

I then went back into the courtroom and joined my other wedding party. When we were called, I again entered the chapel. This time, there was a best man and a bridesmaid in the party. The person performing the service looked at me with a sign of recognition, and I smiled at him. The service was brief, and again I signed off as the witness.

We all met after the service and I was invited to a local bar for a celebration. I declined regretfully, because in truth, I was dressed too casually, and did not feel I fitted in. However, what an experience for me to have been part of! It was memorable in a big way.

When I returned home, there was a large bouquet of flowers waiting for me in the lobby from Tom and Susan. We wrote to each other over the years.

I should like to remind you that in those days there were no legal Gay weddings in New York. This was a Gay wedding in every way as Katie was a lesbian and Willie was gay! It was a marriage of convenience so that he eventually could become a citizen of the United States. They stayed married, in touch, and good friends all through the years, though they did not live together.

Willie and his partner, George, eventually moved to Canada where they lived happily ever after. Not really, because Willie's alcoholism was taking its toll. George was a college professor and Willie did catering as long as he could. They found living in Canada was easier for them at that time, as they were more accepted socially. In his letter Willie wrote, "We're getting by by the skin of our teeth, but at least in Canada the welfare and health systems can ease the situation more than in the U.S., but it is no real compensation or solution."

LONNY'S FRIEND KERA

Kera was one of Lonny's best friends. She was from Australia, too. She was blonde, beautiful and bright.

Lonny and Kera were very close friends and lovers. They toured Europe together. Kera was able to convince Lonny to perform in "Broken Toys," the aforementioned Off-Broadway show that she was in.

We met on several occasions and became friends. Kera would call me on Mother's Day and say, "You are my mother in America!"

Kera lived a very comfortable life. She earned a good living as a high-priced call girl.

One day in 1986, Lonny called me excitedly to tell me that Kera was being interviewed on a news program that day, and that I should listen in. I did better than that. I taped the program on a VHS tape.

It was a special feature on an independent news channel. It was referred to as "Confessions of a High-Priced Call Girl." There was Kera, looking lovely in a black wig, being interviewed. She was sitting on the sofa of her apartment with her legs curled up under her demurely.

<u>Interviewer</u>: Why are you a call girl?

<u>Kera</u>: It's one way to make quite a lot of money without any particular skills.

<u>Interviewer</u>: What does an escort girl really do?

<u>Kera</u>: Sex with clients. The first thing you do is get the business part out of the way. You take the money in cash or a credit card. Then you wait for them to make the first move, unless they are painfully shy. Then I take over. I don't really love what I have to do, but it really doesn't bother me.

<u>Interviewer</u>: Have you ever had a close call with danger?

Kera: Not really.

Interviewer: Do you enjoy your work?

Kera: No, though I find it a lot easier than being a waitress or a bartender.

Interviewer: Do you have to pretend to enjoy it?

Kera: You have to pretend if you can't stand somebody. If they're obnoxious or whatever, you just find something about them that's charming.

Interviewer: Do you know the number of men that you have slept with?

Kera: The last time I counted I was about eighteen. I counted with my sister about one hundred, and that doesn't include work.

Interviewer: Do you consider yourself promiscuous?

Kera: No.

Interviewer: Because you earn about $1000 a night, are you a rich woman?

Kera: No, but I can afford to do whatever I want. If I want to go to London, or take time off from work, I don't have to get permission.

Interviewer: In a perfect world, what would you be doing for a living?

Kera: Nothing. I would be supported by a generous benefactor, who would only want to see me once every six months.

After the interview is over:

Interviewer: Kera's life boasts few signs of wealth. Half her income goes to the Escort agency for whom she works. Her small apartment is far from luxurious. Her clothes look worn....

After some time, she moved up the ladder in that profession. She became a Madam.

In 1989 we received a picture postcard from Kera. She had moved to Brazil. After that she returned to Australia and established herself, and did very well, in a new profession as a home decorator. It was a new way for her to display her talent in business.

LONNY THE DRUG DEALER

Lonny was living in a perfect location for his new occupation. He was good-looking, charming, fun-loving, articulate and well-liked, appropriate personal traits for selling his product. He was finally succeeding in life in his new vocation as a drug dealer.

He had access to all the popular clubs in the city. He never had to wait on line. He would walk up to the bouncers, give them a "hand-off" (money or drugs), and walk right in with confidence like any "big wig" or movie star.

He was still a caring person, generous to his friends and those who needed help. I was told of the time he housed some prostitutes in his apartment on Twelfth Street because they were being mistreated by their pimp. He also allowed them to entertain their Johns there. That building was hopping!

Lonny dealt drugs from a room in that same apartment. His customers would line up outside the door and down the staircase. He hired a big bruiser who would send the buyers in one at a time. Lonny conducted his business with them and off they flew. That building was really hopping!

He tried to keep the operation running smoothly and quietly so as not to disturb the neighbors. From what I learned subsequently, the neighbors were very disturbed and very fed up. They complained to the landlord who decided to finally take action. However, it was a long time until they would be able to rid themselves of Lonny and his thriving enterprise.

With his acuity and surprisingly good business sense, he quickly worked his way to the top of the Drug Dealing hierarchy. In his "dealer days" he had it all – pretty girls, an endless stream of friends, satisfied clients, and a boat load of money. Though he remained in the same small cheap East Village apartment, the rent was $365 monthly, he never denied himself anything and lived the life of a rock star. He once told me, after he moved to Florida and we were spending a lot of time together, that that was the best time in his life. It was the only time that he felt he had made something of himself. He saw himself as a failure in his young life, and now he had achieved something great – Lonny, Kingpin Drug Dealer!

With the cash flowing in and out, things were looking up for Lonny.

When my husband and I were touring Europe, we were in Angers, a town southwest of Paris. We were sitting outside a café enjoying the lovely day. As I gazed down the street, loping towards us was a young man. That young man was our dear Lonny! Out of nowhere, there he was. We couldn't have been more surprised and happy when he decided to join us on the tour.

Lonny was a person of means and he was very generous. He wined and dined his friends and at that time there were many.

He was a Kingpin on a "High" throne. When he fell off, it was as low as you can go.

Lonny, the interloper, surprises us at a café in Angers, France.

Lonny joins us in our tour of France and adds some "Ooh, La La!"

LONNY THE DRUG ADDICT

How to go from Super Dealer to Super Addict – munch on your merchandise more, and more, and more. Munching finally lead to mainlining. Mainlining lead to....

From rock star to addict, Lonny became the scourge of his neighbors, his landlord and Twelfth Street. The zonked out, zombie-like addicts gathered there day and night. They clustered in the street and in the building. It's hard to sympathize with landlords, but Lonny's was to be pitied. The landlord couldn't evict him, much as he tried. He had a ten year lease. Finally, after much agony, time and a two week court trial, he finally succeeded. Lonny was homeless.

It fell upon us, my husband and me, to clean up his apartment. What a traumatic experience that was.

How does one dispose of drug paraphernalia and a beloved Persian cat? It was a quickie lesson in Drugs 101 and a neighbor's compassion for cats.

It should be mentioned here that while he was Lonny, the Druggie, he was being stalked by a New York City policeman. He took advantage of Lonny's weakened and stoned state, physically and mentally. This sadistic person would call me on the telephone at home, after he beat him up, to report how he was "looking after him". Lonny described how he looked after him, and I was horrified. One time, he shot a gun near his ear, and Lonny heard the ringing sound for a long time afterwards. He physically abused him and threatened him with arrest, but there was nothing we could do about it. This police officer claimed he was only doing his job, while he was brutally abusing my son.

There were two occasions that Lonny came up to us in Riverdale for physical help. He had been badly beaten up on the street, I think by another drug dealer. One time he had a broken jaw that had been treated in the hospital. The other time his ribs had been broken. How my heart hurt to see his badly bruised body. He was in so much pain that he felt most comfortable lying on the floor. We were hoping that we could help him to heal, and in the process attempt to detox him. We tried. He stayed for a few days, but needless to say, it didn't happen. How could we have succeeded when we would later find out that several rehab centers had failed?

How shocked we were when we first learned that Lonny was a drug addict. After all, we were a Jewish middle-class family living in an upscale neighborhood. How naive we were, never suspecting, never recognizing the signs. I think he wanted so much to shield us from knowing the dangers of his lifestyle because he loved and respected us.

Later on, when he was in deep decline, he tried not to ask us for monetary help, and he never stole from us. However, he did go begging to our friends. They would tell us that they gave him money and, of course, we would reimburse them. It was an indirect form of enabling that we, the families of addicts, found ourselves in. Typically, parents of addicts are "enabling" when they break down, so overwhelmed with pity and love, and give in to their child's requests for money.

It is then you begin to really understand how hopeless the situation has become.

LONNY'S LOVES

During this period, Lonny was seriously in love, at least two times that I know of.

Sherrie and Lonny loved each other very much. They decided that they wanted to marry. She was a ward of her uncle, a member of a popular singing group. On several occasions, I was on the phone with his wife discussing arrangements for a wedding. However, one should not make future plans when a drug addict is involved, in this case two drug addicts. Many of them develop health issues as a result of their addiction.

Sherrie was taken to the hospital with a stomach ailment. We went to visit her on two occasions. She grew progressively worse and was soon dead. She had died in Lonny's arms. As far as I know, that was the closest Lonny had ever gotten to getting married.

Mara and Lonny were also very much in love. They were inseparable. They were also heavily addicted. Matt, his brother, always looking out for him, offered him a job in Los Angeles. However, he would have to clean up first. He had him admitted to a prestigious drug rehab, one used by celebrities. My husband and I flew out hoping to be of help. We visited him in rehab and he seemed to be doing so well, coherent, happy, and focused on sobriety!

Unfortunately, the lovebirds could not be separated, so Matt, with some influence, was able to get Mara admitted to the program, too. She now joined Lonny as a patient at the rehab center. They lasted all of two days, and decided they didn't need help. The two "drug birds" flew the rehab coop! They left rehab and immediately sought out the closest drug dealer. The three of them returned to their motel room where he robbed them of all their money and possessions. The drug dealer then trashed their room and left. The police were called, and they were evicted and quickly returned to New York to resume life as usual.

Mara also became very ill, her organs destroyed by drug use. When we went to see her in the hospital, we were horrified to see the condition she was in. She was wasting away. What stayed in my mind were her long talon-like fingernails and her yellow skin color. She, too, died in Lonny's arms.

Lonny had more loves to come…..

HIGH HOPES

Excerpt from a letter from a Narcotics Anonymous group in a community center in East Village:

August 5, 1986

To Whom It May Concern:

This is to verify that Lon Lichtenberg has been attending Narcotics Anonymous meetings since 7/27/86. He has also been actively seeking our help in attaining placement in a residential treatment facility. On his release from the hospital, we plan on placing him in one of the facilities in the area.

It is my professional opinion that Mr. Lichtenberg is seriously seeking help with his drug problem, and that given this help he will be a contributing member of his community.

Sincerely yours,

Jim Burns

Everyone was so hopeful, but it was still all up to Lonny!

As far as we knew, Lonny was accepted in at least three rehab centers. As mentioned, we visited the one in California, which was like a country club. He didn't think he needed it, or more likely his drug supply was cut off, so he left.

Later on, we were so grateful when he was accepted by a rehab center near the East River in Manhattan. Of course, we went to visit him there. We hoped this program would be successful, but it wasn't. Lonny had not yet reached the nadir of his life, and so again he ran away. That time was yet to come, the time when he would be living in a refrigerator carton on a street in Manhattan. By then, fortunately, we had moved to Florida.

For the mother of an addict and for his family, life

is one traumatic experience after another. On several occasions, I had to go to court to plead for him. I went to meetings with counselors, joined N.A. groups made up of family members of addicts, and made futile attempts to get him into programs. We visited him in the hospital when he was battered and bruised. We suffered his indignities and pain along with him when we were aware of them.

The first and most important thing that members of the addict's family are taught is not to be an "enabler". As I mentioned before, this means that any requests for help monetarily, or in other ways, have to be turned down. Breaking ties with this very much beloved person affected my health and my life. I was told by my doctor that I had to leave the scene. In 1988, I gave up my teaching job prematurely, and my husband and I packed everything and we moved to Florida. We bought a condo that was listed in The New York Times. Lonny was "out of sight", but he was never "out of mind." We kept in touch with some of his friends who kept us abreast of what they knew about him, but for own well being not too often.

We exchanged correspondence with Willie, one

of Lonny's dearest friends. In 1988 this is what he wrote to us:

> "Kera saw Lonny the other day, still quite desperate so it seems, and forever hopeful nonetheless that he can and will channel that will of his into patience and commitment."

In 1990 He wrote:

> "Kera spoke of seeing Lonny. No doubt, all our hearts are with him, for what that is worth, as things get worse instead of better; our hearts and hope are with you, also."

Fortunately, we were in Florida enjoying the sun when Lonny finally hit bottom.

A LETTER FROM RICHARD

Sept. 16, 1991

To: The Lichtenberg Family:

Dear Mrs. Lichtenberg,

I am writing this note to let you know that Lon was sentenced "on the 13th of this month, on a case he had pending.

I know Lon for almost ten years and I rented him a room in my apartment because I trust him a lot.

The problem is that he does not listen to anyone. His counselor Mr. H., also tried to help him; but he doesn't take his advice.

I am afraid that he will have to learn the way I did. Drugs make good people do crazy things.

Lon is a good person, and sometimes people that are good with others, neglect to be good to themselves.

Please write me if you find out where he is, so I can write to him and send him money. He is going to need money for cigarettes and other things-also money in jail is important because he may be able to buy some "friends."

"Buy friends" means he can help prisoners that are too poor to buy their own things; and when you are in jail is good to have as many friends as you can get.

I will try to keep his room for him, so when he comes out he will have a place to live. Also call his brother in N.Y. and maybe he can also help.

Lon is going to need everyone's help. Now more than ever.

May the blessings of God be with you.

Yours Truly

Richard

Lonny stayed with Richard for a short while. After leaving Richard, he would move in with anyone who would tolerate him and his sometimes dangerous behavior. Finally, there was nobody left, so he took to the streets.

SINKING LOWER

Lonny found a place to live on the lower East Side on Avenue C. It has since been gentrified, but in those days it was known as Drug Alley. It was lined with dingy tenements and the empty lots were strewn with rubble. The neighborhood was gritty and dangerous, and drugs were sold openly.

When he moved on from there to the Bowery, it was a move to more available drugs and sights of deep depths of depravity. He described to a friend what he viewed from the window of his dilapidated flat as he looked across into the slummy holes that were once apartments in the building across from him. He saw acts of sadomasochism and other aberrant sexual behavior. There were "dead to the world" bodies strewn in the courtyard amongst the garbage that lay around. He was often threatened with violence.

It was so horrific that he thought he was hallucinating. That was yet to come.

Alan, Lonny's brother, was on the Fourteenth Street Station of the New York City subway when he noticed a pathetic looking panhandler sitting on the floor in the middle of the platform. He had a sign that said, "I'm Homeless, Hungry and HIV Positive. Please Help Me." He realized that he was looking at his own brother, and getting over the initial shock he picked him up, threw the sign in the trashcan and led him out of the subway. He took him to a local eatery and ordered food for him. Lonny fell asleep at the table, and Alan made a phone call.

Alan was a real estate attorney. He called a client, a fine foreign gentleman, who owned hotels in Manhattan. Out of the kindness of his heart and out of respect for Alan, he gave Lonny a room in a single room occupancy hotel, rent free with meals included. Alan took him right over and set him up in the room. Each day a tray of food was left at his door. Would you believe that Lonny complained that the food was not to his taste?

It was not too long afterwards that Alan received

a phone call from his client asking him to come in and see him. Regretfully, he told him that Lonny had burnt up three of the rooms he had occupied. He was not sure if it was a smoking mishap or it happened while preparing his drugs.

Alan's client offered to move him to his main hotel where he lived with his family, so that he could watch over him. How grateful we were. He tried, but his good intentions did not work out as Lonny declined further.

Imagine, we were hoping for him to hit bottom, so that maybe he would be motivated to finally fight off the drug demon!

A LETTER FROM LONNY - 1991

Dear Mom and Dad,

Words cannot describe how I feel. I wish you could feel what has been going through my head. What happened to me in N.A. terms is called "relapse." I have been going to meetings, hanging around positive people who understand what happened to me. You may not believe this, but I still want my sobriety. That is why I am going to jail, kick my methadone, and come out a different person.

Don't worry. You will get your $1500.00 back.

I hurt you and I am sorry, but try to have a little patience. It's a 15 year disease that is even harder than I expected it to be.

I feel that you, as my parents, instead of throwing me away, especially now, since I am in such a vulnerable situation, should be more understanding, and be a little more tolerant. I just went through three months of pretty intense treatment. I fell off twice in the three months. That's a lot better than getting high every day of my life. I learned a lot in that place. There is no way I can prove anything to you. Time will tell.

Whether you believe it or not, I asked you for survival money. Between you, Alan and Matt, I don't feel it was a lot I asked for. My own family put me in a situation that is so degrading, yet it does not seem to bother any of you. I realize I did this to myself, but if there is any time I need support, it is now. I am doing everything I can to stay clean. I have every reason in the world to get high now, but I have chosen not to. I realize how I f--d up, but life goes on. I must keep fighting my disease.

Instead of being so negative, try a little positive attitude. Anyway, again, I'm sorry I hurt you. You both mean more to me, than I do to myself. I love you and will do my best to prove to you, and me, that there is hope. God bless you.

Love,

Lon

RIKER'S ISLAND

I think he really believed and meant what he wrote in this letter. He lied to us when he had to in order to protect us. In that period of his life, he committed what I like to call "COO," the crime of omission, which was most of the time.

Imagine the ambivalent feelings and agony we felt receiving this letter. He was really desperate because he was sentenced to spend time in Riker's Island jail.

Riker's Island is New York City's largest jail complex. Through the years, it has been known for abuses – drug trafficking, rape, assaults on inmates by guards and other inmates, physical neglect, and publicized scandals.

In the time that Lonny spent there, conditions were

much worse. He was in terrible physical condition. He was slight of build and weakened from the side effects from his use of drugs and detoxing. What were his chances of surviving Riker's Island?

He survived!

He did not want to share with us the sordid details of the time he spent there. When I asked him to tell me about it, to spare me, he would only say that he made sure to make friends with the right people, and he did. One of his friends later told me that a big bully took a liking to him because Lonny made him laugh, and he protected him all through his stay there. That's what kept him alive!

Lonny loved life, and would fight to the end! That we learned later.

LONNY'S HEALTH ISSUES

Lonny was very fortunate that he was being treated, when needed, by a hospital in Manhattan. They detoxed him on occasion, and their caring staff was always there for him.

In 1989 he was diagnosed with HIV positive. This was no surprise. It came as a result of his drug addicted lifestyle, mainly from the sharing of syringes.

Having the HIV virus damages the immune system, and can eventually lead to AIDS, which at that time was a death sentence, and still can be. Victims suffered horrific side effects before they succumbed. At that time people feared those afflicted, and they were shunned.

Fortunately, new tests, treatments and technological

advances were greatly to improve the prognosis of an HIV positive patient. The hospital was running a clinical trial, and Lonny became a part of it. He was given the new medications and was tested on a regular basis. His T cells were normal thereafter.

Thanks to that hospital and their wonderful and patient staff for keeping Lonny alive for the twenty-five years that followed.

According to his medical records Lonny also suffered from other ailments - hepatitis C, myelopathy (spinal cord injury) and neuropathy in his legs. He was in constant pain, and was taking a great deal of medication. There is also mention of Acute Schizophrenic Break, drug aberrant behavior, anxiety and psychosis.

He was being treated for hearing voices and hallucinations. When you hallucinate you see, hear, smell, taste or feel something that is not there. You truly believe that it is happening. Hallucinations can be substance induced, and can happen when drugs are being taken or during withdrawal.

Lonny heard voices and saw the "little people." It is referred to as the Lilliputian Hallucination. This was reported to me by some friends who were present with him when a hallucination was happening.

He said, "Lonny saw the "little people" coming towards him through the walls of his apartment and in the mirrors. He was so convinced and convincing that one of his friends believed that he saw them, too. It was a frightening scene. He was so scared that he kept a knife near his bed in his New York apartment."

Matt was driving with him in a taxi in Manhattan when Lonny was hallucinating. They were on the way to the doctor's office for a routine visit. Lonny saw the "little people" coming out of the walls of the skyscrapers and climbing up and down like Spiderman. These "little people" were swinging from building to building, as the taxi drove along. Lonny described them so visually and in such detail, that you had to believe that he believed what he saw. It was very frightening for Matt and the taxi driver, who could not wait to arrive at their destination. Surprisingly, Lonny was able to dismiss the episode and walked into the doctor's office with a perfectly normal demeanor. Matt and the taxi driver had to be sedated.

Having been a heavy smoker, Lonny developed

C.O.P.D., Chronic Obstructive Pulmonary Disease, which with his other accompanying illnesses greatly affected his lifestyle later on.

Due to the constant, intense and chronic pain Lonny suffered, he was kept on a high dose of methadone for the rest of his life. Methadone does not help addicts get better. It is merely a replacement drug that is controlled in dosage. Owing to its long duration of action, its effectiveness in controlling pain, and its very low cost, it is used in the treatment of drug addiction and other painful ailments. Lonny would always panic if it was not prescribed for him in a timely manner.

As the years passed his health deteriorated, especially his C.O.P.D. condition, and his pain persisted and worsened.

A LETTER FROM LONNY-1993

Dear Mom & Dad,

Hi. Hope you're feeling good.

I'm writing you because I'm not allowed to call you till I'm out of orientation. That will be for another three weeks.

Things are going good here. They are going to give me a treatment plan at the end of the week. I'm now on my fourth week detoxing. It should not be too bad. I came in on a very low dose, 30 M.G. (methadone?). They detox you 10 M.G. every two weeks, so I should be off the line by the end of August. I'm not expecting it to be too bad. Not like it was when I was in jail.

I am in a house with sixty-five other drug abusers. All of them were on methadone programs. All of them have been detoxed within a period of seven months. Mine is short because of my low dose.

It gets pretty hectic having sixty-five different personalities in one facility, but you get used to it. There are about six other people here with the HIV virus. We go to a support group once a week. All of them get two hours a day of bed rest, except for me. My test results came back so good, they refuse me bed rest. Isn't that great news? Sometimes I get real tired, so when I do, I go to Staff and ask them if I can lie down. They usually don't deny me.

I have a counselor. If you have any questions, you can call and talk to her. I'm pretty sure I'm allowed one incoming call, so if you want, drop a line. I tried to get permission to call Matt, but was denied. I have to wait till I am out of orientation.

That's all for now. You probably won't hear from me for another three weeks. Don't worry. Everything is going great. Give my love to everybody. I'm looking forward to the day we can be together, me being drug free.

I love you very much.

      Your Son,

      Lonny

1993
Lonny, Matt, and Frank and I
are on the town.
It's visiting day at the rehab center.

THE BIG DAY ARRIVES - 1994

Lonny had always had a zest for living and enjoying life. After Riker's Island with its unspeakable conditions, the painful detoxing, and thereafter living on the street, he realized he had hit bottom and was ready to fight his drug addiction.

He was again accepted by another rehab facility, a residential substance abuse center in Queens, New York. Its main effort is to eradicate the devastating effect of substance abuse on the individuals, their families and their loved ones by helping those addicted take on the responsibility for their own recovery.

Lonny's letter describes the routine of the early part of his stay there. He shared living quarters with twelve people in one very large room. Each had his own bed, dresser and closet. They also shared a common goal, to get back to their lives, their loves, their family and friends.

Making friends was very easy for him. It is no surprise that there was a mutual attraction between Lonny and a young lady who was in the program. The relationship never developed as romance was not one of the twelve steps.

During his stay, my husband and I, and Matt went to New York to visit Lonny. We took him out for the day accompanied by his counselor. He looked well-groomed, healthier and was very optimistic about his future. As we dined at a local restaurant, he was the fun-loving Lonny that we once knew. When we left him and returned to Florida, though we were happy, it was with guarded expectations.

After about eighteen months at the rehab facility, the big day that we were waiting and hoping for, arrived. We were invited to his graduation on September 24, 1994, at a local college. My husband and I flew in from Florida, and Matt from California. The college auditorium was filled with families and friends happily waiting for the program to begin. I was very touched and filled with hope during the graduation ceremony. As each name was called, the graduates proudly walked across the stage, while our voices cheered and our eyes teared. We were high on high hopes.

We celebrated with the family and friends afterwards, and returned back home to Florida. Lonny was ready to begin his life anew.

1994
Rehab Graduation Day-
Drug free at last!

MORE LETTERS - 1996

Letter from Lonny:

Dear Willie,

How are you? I'm doing fine. I'm just so glad that you stayed in touch with my family, who loves you very much. I know that you and Kera were very concerned about drugs and HIV. I know that you will be happy to hear that I have been almost four years clean, and my health is very good.

It has been a long time since I saw or spoke to you, and I would like very much to hear from you. I would also like to get in touch with Kera, and if you speak to her, tell her that I love her.

PLEASE get in touch with me. There is so much for us to talk about. I hope all is well with you both.

Love,

Lon

Letter from Willie:

Dear Gloria and Fred,

Great to hear from you, and even greater, to have such good news from Lonny. Have written to him already and also sent Kera a postcard telling her the good news. So many people we've known have been lost to AIDS and the rest, that the news of Lonny, as well as the joy for his recovery, brings a much needed dose of hope and optimism.

A close friend of mine, Valerie, has been HIV positive for some eight years now. She's living life to the full, and doing wonders despite the odds – a lot of work with AIDS patients and drug abusers, continuing with her art and performance work. She's a very positive example (and no doubt there are many more out there) for Lonny.

Having overcome his addiction must have taken as much strength and courage, as it has time. Having found that, there also lies the key to living well with HIV.

Can't wait to see him again, and as things stand, I won't be making it to New York City until Spring,'97. Have offered him an open invitation to visit us here in Montreal, in the meantime, however.

Katie, my wife, was here for a holiday when news of Lonny arrived, so we checked out our old wedding photos, and had a nostalgic return to the better times of the '80's.

No doubt Lonny's recovery has meant an incredible amount to you both. I guess we're all so happy for him; proud of him, but for his mom and dad it must have been wonderful to spend time together once again.

Many thanks for keeping in touch. All the

best, and may Lonny be alive <u>with us</u> for a very long time,

Willie

The wedding photos that Willie refers to are of the Gay wedding that I described earlier in my story.

Lonny sporting a big smile, with his dad, Frank, visiting Matt in California.

LIFE ON EAST SEVENTY-FIRST STREET

While he was seeing someone else, Lonny and Sally were introduced by a friend at a Narcotics Anonymous meeting. The attraction was immediate. She became his love, and helped him deal with his drug demons. She put stability in his life. She would remain his dearest friend for the rest of his life.

His brother, Alan, knew someone who had a realty company, and was able to get them a rent stabilized apartment, a fourth floor walk-up on East Seventy-First Street. It was what is called a railroad flat. It had a long hall with very small rooms. The living room had a giant TV, a sofa, and Sally's chotchkes (collectibles and such). The bedroom was so tiny that they had to use a loft bed, in order to leave room on the floor for furniture. However, they were delighted to have a place of their own in a very nice neighborhood in Manhattan. It was a neat nest for the love-birds.

Sally was the sweetest, kindest, most giving person in Lonny's life. She worked very hard as a delivery person, driving a truck for a large company. However, she had an imperfection. She was a compulsive buyer, and companies like QVC benefited. Between the two of them, they built up those credit bills.

Their pride and joy was Boo, a beautiful Maltese dog. He was their virtual child. I remember Sally describing Boo wearing a lampshade around his neck due to an injury. He was always the subject of conversation in our phone calls.

Lonny finally found a job that he really liked. He was employed by a company that recycled bottles and cans. Each day, the homeless, unemployed, drug addicted, and indigent would do their daily physical activity – picking through trash cans and dumpsters. They were doing their part in cleaning up the streets of New York, and getting their exercise, too!

They would line up with their collections, and Lonny

would give them chits which they would turn in for cash. Because of his kind and sympathetic nature, he related to these unfortunate people. He cheered them up with his happy demeanor, and they looked forward to turning over their finds to him. Lonny made the recycling cans and bottles activity a happy experience in their sad lives.

Lonny was still part of the HIV program at his hospital, and he remained free from AIDS. However, he was a heavy smoker like my husband, Frank, who died from C.O.P.D. Because Lonny's lungs were diseased and his legs caused him constant pain, it was an effort for him to climb to the fourth floor.

Sally's mother lived in Florida, too. They decided to come down and visit us. They loved what they saw - the beaches, the year-round greenery, and a physically easier lifestyle. Living was cheaper, and they would see to it that they would not have to climb stairs.

Sally's back was bothering her, and she was finding her job as a package delivery driver very difficult. Lonny was feeling progressively worse, and was not able to work any longer.

One day, they found that a mouse was making his home in their couch. They decided there was not enough room for the four of them – two adults, a dog and a mouse. It was the mouse that broke the camel's back, and it was time for them to move South.

So it was that Sally and her books and collectibles, Lonny and his medications, and Boo and his lampshade collar moved to sunny Florida.

Oh, My! It's a dog's life wearing a lampshade collar.

FLORIDA, WE'RE HERE!

Lonny and Sally found a bright little apartment on the ground floor in a rental complex in Boynton Beach. They brought with them all their possessions, Boo and their credit card debts. Living in Florida is easier on the wallet, the credit card in their case. Food, services, entertainment, almost everything is there for you at a reasonable price. Owning a car is a necessity, and having a job helps, too.

One of the first things they did was to join a local Narcotics Anonymous chapter. Lonny was very articulate and convincing and he would chair some of the meetings. There they met Greg who greatly impacted both their lives.

Sally tried to find employment with the company she had worked for up North, but there were no openings. It was just as well, because her back was bothering her very much, probably caused by the lifting and carrying necessary for that strenuous job. It was time to move on to something new.

They lived very close to the beach, and went frequently with Boo, who joyfully romped in the sand. Sally loved to swim and sunbathe, and sported a perpetual tan. She was Lonny's brown-skinned beauty, and he was her blue-eyed best buddy. Florida and life were looking good!

Sally had a very caring and supportive family of brothers, nieces and nephews. She was delighted when they came down to visit. On this occasion, they were anticipating a day at the beach. They were in the parking lot loading up the car, Boo jumping and wagging his tail, happy to be with this jovial bunch going to the beach. Everyone piled into the car and they were off.

They were on their way, and it was not long before they realized that Boo was not with them. They had left him in the parking lot. They rushed back, but he was gone. A neighbor later said that she had seen him waiting in front of their apartment door earlier. After that, he must have wandered off.

They searched the neighborhood, local developments, shopping malls, everywhere. They called the police and local animal shelters and they hung posters offering a reward. They received a few calls saying that Boo had been sighted, but they led to nothing. All was to no avail. We imagined the worst scenario, that he had been hit by a car. Hopefully, maybe he was found by a caring dog lover. Sadly, we never learned what happened to Boo!

Lonny and Sally had lost their beloved dog, their virtual child. They never got over it.

Taking the dog by the leash, I offered to gift them with a replacement. They chose another Maltese puppy, Lola, a female. They loved her at first sight, but Boo was never out of their hearts.

Sally was happy to get a job with a landscaping company. She loved plants and enjoyed tending to them. It was more gratifying, by far, than delivering people's packages.

Lonny was too disabled to seek employment. At times, he was taking as many as seventeen medications a day. The HIV was in check, but the C.O.P.D.

was worsening. My husband, Frank, had died the previous year of the same illness. This was a concern for all of us.

The new apartment was small and the rent was going up. Lonny needed a more comfortable living arrangement and a more affordable rent. Matt to the rescue!

Lonny, contemplating
in the Florida sun.

MOVING ON, MOVING IN

Matt decided to buy a condo in Boynton Beach. He could use it as a pied-a-terre, as he had clients that performed in Florida, and Lonny could live in it as the caretaker. In the meantime, Lonny and Lola lived with me for four months.

We shopped around for a condo in modest developments in my area. We found THE perfect place for Lonny and Lola. It was love at first sight, and whatever Lonny and Lola wanted, Lonny and Lola got. It had three bedrooms, two baths and a patio. It was a one story end unit, and was surrounded by trees, bushes and a big lawn. It was always green. When you looked out of the window or were on the patio, you were greeted with green.

Best of all, it was dog friendly, a great way to meet

your neighbors. Lonny met his cul-de-sac neighbors and Lola met their dogs. While dog walking, he met Noreen and Lola met Sam. They became very important in Lonny's and Lola's lives.

Lonny and I went furniture shopping. He was still mobile, and was able to drive and move around with the aid of puffers. We both agreed on the style and colors, and we were able to find attractive and functional furniture for all the rooms at reasonable sale prices. We found paintings for the walls, a rug and a beautiful dining room set at Faith Farm.

We set up a computer corner. There he expanded his interests and busied himself. As the outside world became more inaccessible, the computer opened another world that allowed him to make many friends and enjoy life.

For him, the most important purchase was a fifty inch TV and a sound system for his bedroom, where he eventually ended up spending most of his time.

Lonny was more than contented with his new showplace. He had someone take care of the bushes and plants outside the entrance, and added garden ornaments. They were a welcoming to Lonny and Lola's lair!

As you might be wondering, someone is conspicuous by her absence. Unbeknownst to me, Sally and Lonny had a falling out. She left him and moved in with a friend who lived near the beach, which she dearly loved. I never learned why they parted, but they remained loving friends, and she was always there when he needed her, and when she needed him.

I learned later that when Sally and Greg met, they fell in love with each other, and eventually moved into his cozy apartment near the beach.

Despite the physical rift, they were still the best of friends. They were like the Three Musketeers, and Sally, Greg and Lonny were always there for each other.

Biding Time at My House-
Lola, and Lonny wearing a Yankee shirt, white socks and a wide nicotine gum smile!

SETTLING IN

At this point in his life Lonny, was still able to get around by himself. His home was located near a very busy shopping area. He particularly enjoyed food shopping at the local supermarket. He would pour over the weekly ads, and was attracted to the BOGO's, Buy One Get One Free. Except for coffee and a few other items, he would give the "one free" to me or his friends. His kitchen cabinet was full to the brim with packages of BOGO coffee.

It was most important for him to set up his medical care. In New York City, he was very well-taken care of by the doctors at his hospital. In Florida, again he was fortunate to be serviced by physicians who were competent and available to him when he needed them. As time passed, that need grew!

Together, we found organizations that could be of help to him. The American Lung Association held monthly meetings that we attended. It was an education for both of us. They made suggestions for living with C.O.P.D. that were helpful, and we learned about the available equipment that he would eventually be using.

CAP, The Comprehensive Aids Program of Palm Beach County, provides education and assistance to AIDS patients and their families. They directed Lonny to services that were available. His case worker arranged for him to get Home Health Care assistance. We were very grateful for their input and assistance.

The aides were all competent and pleasant, except for one. When Lonny asked her to feed Lola once a day she replied, "I don't feed dogs." To Lonny, Lola wasn't just a dog, she was his life! P.S. – the aide ended up going to the dogs.

Since I am a dog lover, there is nothing wrong with that!

Out for Dinner in Florida -
Alan, Matt and I with wide toothy smiles, and Lonny is just smiling.

SETTLED IN

Sally, the kind and caring person she was, remained Lonny's dear friend. She would check in with him almost every day and bring him his daily dose of Dunkin' Donuts coffee. Of course, he started the day earlier with a cup of his own BOGO name brand or the supermarket variety.

Sally was now working as a landscaper. She would bring him plants that were dying, with the hope that he would resuscitate them, and he did. He enjoyed caring for them. He really had a green thumb, which came in handy, as you will read later. Sally brought me some beautiful plants, too, some of which are still alive today. When I sit on my patio, I feel like I am living in a greenhouse.

Lonny ALWAYS wore white socks. He wore them

around the house without shoes, and with sneakers and shoes when he went out. He was very fussy about his white socks and kept them in a neat pile in his drawer. He was addicted to them, and they were the first thing on his shopping list when he thought they were running low.

Lonny's neighbors were very congenial, especially the ones with dogs. Noreen was his best neighbor friend. She lived in another cul-de-sac, but it could be reached by walking across a wide expanse of grass. She had a dog named Sam. It was love at first sight for Lola and Sam.

Noreen worked hard at her job while bringing up a teen-aged daughter. She always found time to check in with Lonny. They would set up play dates for the two dogs. It was a joy to watch the two of them romping around. Noreen was going to play an important part in Lonny's life when he needed help later on.

He doted on Lola. She had her regular grooming sessions and vet visits. Eventually Lola's groomer would come to the house. Unfortunately, vet visits were too frequent because Lola had a skin allergy. Her skin would break out and she would be very uncomfortable. She was put on a special diet and medications that were very costly. The condition never stopped recurring. What we needed was Obama Care for dogs!

Lola had her definitive likes and dislikes. For some reason she did not like the oxygen delivery fellow. She barked loudly before he came in, attacked him, and it looked like she was going to take a nip out of him. One time, I think she did. She was so small and here she was going at this big guy and terrifying him. Lonny couldn't hold back his laughter. It wasn't really funny, and he had to set things straight and promise to lock Lola in another room when the delivery guy was expected.

Lola liked Sue, our housekeeper. She would often bring "dog delicious" meals for Lola, who always displayed such delight when she saw her, and even more so when she was eating her home cooked dishes. It was no wonder she preferred Sue to me. How could my picking up her poop compare to the joy of eating a home-cooked stew? Too bad I wasn't a better cook!

I don't think that Lola liked me too much. I am a dog lover and usually the feeling is reciprocated. Not so in Lola's case. She was so adorable and I wanted so much to cuddle her on my lap. I would forcibly hold her down but she would wiggle and try to jump off. As soon as Lonny or Alan sat down on another part of the couch, she bounded away from me, jumped on their lap and snuggled contentedly. What a blow to my dog ego! Is it possible that in some cases female dogs like male humans better?

Lonny had been a very heavy smoker. He finally had to give it up because of his C.O.P.D. He then became addicted to nicotine gum which is costly, and cough drops which are not. He panicked if he ran out. He was also taking prescribed methadone for his pain. He was a pain to his doctor when the prescription was late in coming. I believe that he still had some addict left in him!

He had a drug relapse on two occasions. A visiting friend brought some heroin with him. Lonny succumbed, but after two days he was able to control himself with the methadone. The same thing happened another time, but he realized that it was endangering his poor health further and he stopped, never to relapse again. Besides, he always had the methadone.

Lonny was having a problem with his teeth, probably due to a combination of his past lifestyle and heredity. I had never seen my parents with their original teeth because they always wore dentures. The discomfort and pain became too much for Lonny. When the dentist suggested implants for his whole mouth, Lonny told him to pull them all out and make dentures for him.

So began his life as a denture-wearer. He hated them! He was uncomfortable wearing them, so he rarely wore them at home, and sometimes did not wear them when he went out. We became accustomed to his handsome young face with an old man's mouth.

He loved food, particularly filet mignon. It was a matter of gumming it or suffering the pain while chewing with dentures. I think the gumming was winning out.

He did not give up and tried a new set of dentures. He had the same problems. There was going to be a third, and last set, that he made sure to have for a very special occasion, my birthday.

Chilling out at Chez Lonny -
Alan, Lola, and Lonny wearing a
Yankee shirt, white socks and a toothless smile.

LOLA AND THE NOT SO FRIENDLY SKIES

It was a "flight from hell" for Lonny, Lola and me. It started when we arrived at the airport and discovered that our driver had not loaded Lola's pet carrier into the car. There was no time to go back and retrieve it. I did not panic because they usually can be rented at the airport desk. This time they did not have any available. We were able to buy a human carry-on at the airport store. It was acceptable to the airline and we paid the $80 extra for the dog hoping that we would be comfortably seated.

Not so. Our row was occupied by three adults and Lola. We were immediately advised by the stewardess that Lola MUST remain in this black airless bag for the whole trip. Being a not so dumb dog, she didn't want to stay in it. After pushing herself out of the bag, being a well-behaved sweetie she sat placidly squeezed between us, not making a sound. We really tried to conform and forced her back into the bag, but each time she would push herself out.

We did not feed her or give her water. We and the gentleman next to us did not move out of our seats for the whole trip. We were told that it was an FAA ruling and we accepted, understood and tried to abide by it but Lola, the guilty party, did not understand. We were visited by the supervisor who reinforced the ruling with more finality. We were approaching our destination as we stuffed her into the bag again holding her down. This time there was no struggle.

Lola got her revenge. She did not make a peep, she made a poop! We left that despicable black bag on the seat and hurried off the plane.

Whatever Lola wants, Lola gets -
and sometimes NOT!

BANKRUPTCY

A fundamental goal of the federal bankruptcy laws enacted by Congress is "to give debtors a financial 'fresh start' from burdensome debts." The Supreme Court made this point about the purpose of the bankruptcy law in a 1934 decision:

"It gives to the honest but unfortunate debtor....a new opportunity in life and a clear field for future effort, unhampered by the pressure and discouragement of preexisting debt."

Lonny decided it was time for him to free himself of his burdensome debts! He was unable to meet his rent, and he was tired of his mailbox being clogged up with bills from the collection agencies. He was going to do what the "Big Guys" do - go into bankruptcy.

Lonny consulted with an attorney and was advised to write letters to all of his creditors as follows:

Dear Sirs:

I am in receipt of your most recent bill. This letter will formally describe my current situation.

I am unable to pay all or any portion of the debt. I own no assets of any kind other than my personal property. I have no bank accounts of any kind, except for a single checking account the current balance of which is twenty-five dollars.

Be it known that your efforts and practices to collect this debt have had severe, significant and negative impact on my health, leading to deterioration of my condition. I ask that you stop immediately to prevent further injury to me.

Without charge or payment of any kind, I have received the assistance of an attorney in the drafting of this letter.

>Very truly yours,
>
>Lon Lichtenberg

He sent out this letter to all his creditors, but with no results. He was "an honest but unfortunate debtor", so he made up his mind to finally do something about it. He would go into bankruptcy, Chapter Seven. He did his research on the internet and started to put his financial matters in order. He was required to take a federally mandated credit counseling course within six months of the filing. He breezed through the course , received his Certificate of Debtor Education and filed for Chapter Seven.

Lonny was incapable of going to the final hearing at the courthouse, so Alan and I went. The room was packed with people with the same purpose, hoping for a fresh start. We were called in and the process was completed.

It was like a divorce without alimony! Free at last! Never again!

T.V. OR NOT T.V.

Lonny's C.O.P.D. was getting worse. He was now on oxygen twenty-four hours a day. If he had to leave the house for a doctor's visit, or for any other reason, he carried a portable tank with him. The huge oxygen tank in his living room had long breathing tubes so that they could reach every room. They would become tangled up and block the air flow, and sometimes Lola would use them for "paw play." Those tubes were easy to trip over. Just ask me!

The tank had to be replaced about every week. Sometimes there was a delivery problem. How we would sweat through that. Fortunately, Lonny was always so cheerful and pleasant that he was well-liked by the people who serviced him. That gave him something of an edge in that department. He would get his oxygen delivery!

I was visiting him more often, almost every day. He had the aide in the morning, so I would come afterwards. Someone had to walk Lola in the afternoons and tend to Lonny's other needs. His cheerful personality made it a pleasure to be with him. Despite his disabilities, he still found joy in being alive.

Sometimes I could hear him laughing in the other room. He would be listening to the Howard Stern Show on Sirius radio. Lonny was furious when Howard went to Sirius and he would have to pay to listen to him, but he did. He could describe every oddball character on the show, as if he could see them. I don't think he could have ever foreseen Howard's new persona as a serious judge on America's Got Talent. I think he would have loved him that much more!

We frequently watched TV, he in bed and I on his rocker. His favorite show in this whole world was The Steve Wilkos Show. Steve is a former police officer who tries to resolve his guests' problems and disagreements. The show would run lie detector tests or paternity tests on the accused cheater or abuser. The guests sometimes became violent and Big Steve would have to break up a fight. Lonny thought the show was hilarious, and was a faithful fan for years. I went along for the ride on the rocker.

As a judge of T.V. shows, he chose to watch Judge Judy and Judge Mathis daily. He enjoyed the reality and often comedic aspects of the cases. He was ahead of his time because reality shows are so popular now.

Surprisingly, he had eclectic taste and there were many shows we could watch together and enjoy. He introduced me to Meercat Manor on Animal Planet. This series is about several families of Meercats living in the Kalahari Desert and how they interact for their survival. These little creatures stood on two legs and faced some of the problems that humans do. It was an amazing documentary, and we watched all four seasons--fifty-two episodes.

Lonny was an avid sports fan. He enjoyed watching baseball, football, hockey, basketball and the fights. I think his favorite was MMA – Mixed Martial Arts. Sometimes he would order Pay-Per-View and invite his friends to watch with him on his super-sized screen. They would sit around his bed and enjoy the camaraderie one feels cheering or booing together.

I was with Lonny and Alan on a Super Bowl Sunday when the Giants were playing. It was suggested that we place a bet on the game. It was five minutes before the game started. Alan found a site on the computer and placed the bet just in time. The odds were three to one. It was probably one of the most exciting times in my sports life, especially when the Giants won, and we won, too --$400!

Lonny enjoyed watching re-runs of Seinfeld, one of his favorite programs. He liked to tell about the episode when Jerry visits his parents in Florida. Their plan for the evening is to visit the Lichtenbergs. Ah yes, I remember that evening with the Seinfelds well!

Lola and Lonny -
A dog and her boy!

FRIENDS TO THE END

When Lonny could not walk Lola anymore, arrangements had to be made. His dear friend and neighbor, Noreen, came to the rescue. She walked Lola and her dog Sam every morning before she went to work. She called him whenever she went food shopping to find out what he needed. She returned with the purchases, usually including one or two BOGO's of the week. Noreen, if she was able, was always there when he needed her.

Sally had evolved from Lonny's lover into his loving friend. As mentioned, she regularly checked in with him each morning, Dunkin' Donuts coffee in hand. She, too, had her own problems. Her mother, who lived in Florida, recently had died of cancer and Sally had been diagnosed with the same disease. There was sadness in the air when she was around. Sally died of cancer a year after Lonny.

Greg was a third brother to Lonny. The times he wasn't working, he would spend with him. He was a Mr. Fix-it and kept things running. Lonny was not too handy around the house. They had an affinity for each other. Their eyes would meet, and they would burst out laughing. Greg would run errands for him. He loved Lola too, and sometimes when I was not available, he would take her to the vet. Greg would always be there for Lonny.

Lonny met girlfriends on the internet. Sometimes they were local and would come to visit with him. Debbie would bring her three year old son. Matt was in from California and we invited Debbie out to dinner with us. I remember that she had a very healthy appetite.

I think that Lonny was truly in love with Marlena who lived in Albania. I had never heard much about Albania until there was Marlena. I am skeptical about foreign relationships on the internet because you hear about so many scams. I think Lonny had been scammed once before. Marlena seemed like the real thing. It was for Lonny.

AN INTERVIEW WITH GREG

Greg was Lonny's most intimate and dearest friend. In an interview with him, I tried to emulate the style of a very effective interviewer on television. I am G.L.

G.L.: How would you describe Lonny?

GREG: The first thing that comes to mind is funny, but, of course, he was much more. Lonny was the type of person who would give you the shirt off his back if you needed it, and would never bring it up again. When he gave it, it was unconditional.

He was very street smart. He had been through a lot in his life. You didn't want to get him mad. Most of all he had a great heart, and was very giving.

He was very resourceful. There was a hurricane forecast. Lonny needed electricity for his breathing and his meds. He was determined to get a generator, but the stores were sold out. He saw a guy loading a generator on his truck. He managed to convince him to sell it to him. He was a great convincer!

After the hurricane, with the power gone, we needed ice. He went to different restaurants and loaded up. Then he went around to friends and neighbors and distributed it.

He was very smart (for some reason he didn't think so). He was great at math. When he sent me to the store he would make a list, know how much it cost, what was on sale, Buy One Get One, and of course, he gave me the extra from the BOGO. I would call him when I was at work for his opinion on many different occasions. I valued it very much.

To describe Lonny physically is a must. He was 5'6" or 5'7", thin, a full head of hair, a great smile with a contagious laugh. He had flat feet that gave him that very distinctive walk, and naturally, he was very proud of his "Lichtenshlong". That's what he called his penis because he had a penis bigger than most. He didn't brag. He didn't have to.

<u>G.L.:</u> How did you spend your time with him?

<u>GREG:</u> We would spend a lot of time at his house in the last few years. He felt more comfortable there because of his sickness. I would come over almost every morning for Dunkin' Donuts coffee. If it wasn't the morning, then it was the afternoon. We talked about Howard Stern and Lonny's encounters on the computer. We watched fights on the T.V. or On Demand. Lonny and I did a lot of talking. We were very compatible in the way that we could say anything to each other and it would not be judged. If people were listening, we could have solved the world's problems!

We were so comfortable with each other that we could sit around and say nothing for long periods of time. We were like an episode in a Seinfeld show about nothing.

G.L.: Tell me some funny experiences you had with him.

GREG: We went to the Hard Rock to see the fights. We had seats high up, but in the middle so you could see everything. It was a fun night. We made friends with almost the entire section. Lonny got hit on by what he called a beast. He was used to model types. After the fight, we had to get down from the upper deck. Just imagine him with the helios (small oxygen tank) climbing all the way down. But he still made jokes!

G.L.: Do you remember any sad experiences?

GREG: After Lonny died, I think I blocked out the sad moments. We must have had some, but I can't put them into words.

G.L.: What were some memorable experiences?

GREG: Sally, Lonny and I drove up to Orlando to the Metallica concert. Matt was able to get us all tickets for the show, and backstage as well. We saw Matt there, and he took us into a big tent where they had food, drinks and video games. We met the performers. We had a great time until the drive home. Lonny's legs were hurting him, and he lay in the back of the truck groaning, like he was dying. He still made jokes though. You gotta love him!

G.L.: What T.V. programs did you watch together?

GREG: Boxing, MMA, Jerry Springer, Steve Wilkos, and we listened to HOWARD STERN.

G.L.: You were so close, did you agree on everything?

GREG: Not really, but we did on the things that mattered. I remember the time that Lonny decided he wanted a hand gun. Living alone, he felt vulnerable because of his physical disability, and he wanted to be able to protect himself. I didn't think it was a very good idea and I tried to talk him out of it. As usual, he got his way and we went to a local gun shop. Of course, they wouldn't sell him a gun because of his record. He was so disappointed, but I was so happy! I pictured him nodding off on his couch with his gun beside him. Suddenly the front door opens, he jumps up, and POW! shoots the intruder. What if the intruder turns out to be ME, his best buddy? A gun was definitely out!

G.L.: Why were you his friend?

GREG: He brought me joy. His friendship was unconditional, and we were able to talk about anything.

G.L.: How did he impact or influence your life?

GREG: I DIDN'T KNOW THAT I COULD LOVE A MAN THE WAY I LOVED HIM! He saved my life. One day, I came to Lonny's house after work. We were talking. All at once, I started to sweat like a pig. The water was running down my whole body. Lonny gave me two aspirin and dialed 911. He knew I was having a heart attack. The ambulance tech said that Lonny saved my life with the aspirin. If it was up to me, I would never have called 911. I wouldn't be here today.

G.L.: What made you guys laugh?

GREG: We would laugh at just about anything. Sally was the brunt of a lot of our humor, in a loving way.

G.L.: If you had the chance, what would you say to Lonny?

GREG: Are you okay? Is there anything I can do? Do you see Sally? I miss you!

G.L.: Thank you Greg for your insightful, informative and poignant recollections of my Lonny Love!

POT LUCK

As aforementioned, Lonny and I had the same housekeeper, Sue. She had worked for me for many years and for Lonny the short time that he was living in Florida. She was really nice, thoughtful, eager to help, and a great gardener.

One day, we were on my patio discussing my beautiful plants, which she always takes an interest in.

"Lonny is very good at growing plants, too," said Sue. "He has some beautiful leafy specimen growing inside his house. I really don't know, but they might even be marijuana. You must know about it."

MY SON LONNY, A FELON, GROWING MARIJUANA PLANTS IN FLORIDA!!??

"Oh, no, I didn't know that Lonny might be growing marijuana plants," I gulped.

"Oh, yes, something is flourishing in the walk-in closet in his bedroom," said Sue.

"Sue, why don't you take the rest of the day off. Um, I have something to take care of," I stammered.

No sooner was she out of the door that I was on the phone calling the felon.

I prided myself on not being a prying mother, and I respect privacy. Although I spent time in his bedroom, I did not venture into his walk-in closet because there was never a need for me to do so.

"Hey Lonny, I'm coming right over. I hear there's a surprise for me in your walk-in closet."

When I got there, he greeted me with a guilty, sheepish grin, visibly upset. When I opened the closet, I could not believe what I saw. It looked like he partnered with Jack OF the Beanstalk! Though I did not know marijuana from mint, to me, the plants looked lush and beautiful. They were growing so tall that he had to take down the top shelf of the closet, which was lying on the floor.

He described to me later how much effort he put into the project. He got all his information on the internet. He ordered ten packages of seeds from a company in Sweden. They arrived in a CD case, ten to a package. He had to install very expensive lights which hung from a chain. As the plants grew taller, he had to move the lights higher so they would have room to grow. The lights finally hit the ceiling. He marked each plant and the progress it made. He had a check-in sheet on which he kept his notes. He used a thermometer to keep the closet at 79 to 86 degrees. For this he had a big fan going, as needed. He constantly tested the soil and used bat guano for fertilizer.

He was getting ready for harvest time. That is when you keep the lights on all the time and the plants give off a very strong odor that permeates the whole house. He was afraid that the odor would give away his secret project and he would be in big trouble. This never did happen!

Lonny had something else to fear. He was afraid that there would be a spike in his electric bill because of the intense lighting, and that FPL would want to come to his house and check it out. He turned off the air conditioner and tried to use as little electricity as possible. He even considered buying an air conditioner for his bedroom window. When his friends complained that they were uncomfortable, he would ignore them. However, it was not good for his health either. He himself could not tolerate the heat, and he was forced to turn on the air after awhile.

Lonny tried to explain to me, almost in tears, that this was probably one of the most successful endeavors in his useless life. He had achieved something great, in his own eyes, and he was no longer a failure.

I felt sorry for him and I understood what the marijuana meant to him, but I had to bust the pot bubble! I could not go through what I had in the past. I was afraid to give him the ultimatum, "Either the plants go or I go!" because I had a feeling I knew which he would choose. Instead I snarled, "You have one day to clean up the evidence!" He did.

And so ended Lonny's marijuana misadventure.

I felt a mother's misery again, and it had to be one of the saddest days of Lonny Love's life.

Lonny's cannabis came out of the closet!

PARTY TIMES

In 2010, we celebrated two important birthdays. It was a Big Birthday for me, my eightieth, and Lonny's forty-ninth. It was to be his last.

My sons were going to make me a surprise party. Having had enough surprises in my life, when I learned about it, I became part of the planning. We chose a local catering restaurant that was featuring a very entertaining show. I invited twenty people that had been especially nice to me in special ways. In gratitude, on the invitation I specified that I did not want their presents, just their presence.

The day for my celebration arrived. Alan, Lonny with his small oxygen tank, I and my friends met at the restaurant. When Lonny smiled at me, I was dazzled by his white, wide smile. He was wearing new dentures that he had had made in time for the party, so that he would be sporting a smile in the photos.

When we were all seated, I happened to look up. There was Matt striding across the room towards me. He had come all the way from California. This was one wonderful surprise!

We took great pictures with <u>all</u> of us smiling. There is even a video of Lonny clowning around. On top of my Facebook page, there is a photo of the four of us at the party. It will remain there as long as I do.

Lonny grew tired about halfway through the party, and Alan drove him home.

May twenty-second, 2010, was Lonny's forty-ninth birthday. We planned a barbeque for a few of us. The entrée was filet mignon. That day he wore his dentures!

I wrote a card for him that I framed.

WHO IS LONNY?

WHO IS LONNY, WHAT IS HE?

THE SON WHO SHARES HIS LIFE WITH ME!

HE'S ALWAYS THERE TO LEND A HAND;

MY MANY MOODS HE'LL UNDERSTAND.

A LOVING BROTHER, A FAITHFUL FRIEND,

SOMEONE ON WHOM YOU CAN DEPEND!

GIVE HIM FOOTBALL AND AN EASY CHAIR,

FOR HE'S A SPORTS FAN "EXTRAORDINAIRE"!

KNOWS WORLD AFFAIRS AND THE LATEST NEWS,

A SYMPATHETIC "MENSCH" WITH HIS LIBERAL VIEWS!

LOVES HIS GARDEN AND HOME, BUT HIS PRIDE AND JOY

IS THE BEAUTIFUL LOLA, HIS MALTESE TOY!

WHO IS LONNY AND WHAT IS HE?

SOMEONE WHO MEANS THE WORLD TO ME!

HAPPY BIRTHDAY WITH LOVE,

MOM

It's My Birthday!
Everyone is sporting a wide smile.

THE END IS NEAR

Lonny's health continued to deteriorate. Alan came down from New York to help look after him.

Every so often, Lonny could not catch his breath and he panicked. He would tell Alan in a frightened voice to call 911. This happened at least a dozen times while Alan was staying with him. The medics would arrive and rush him to the hospital. Alan followed behind with an inconspicuous little bag filled with fresh underwear, white socks, nicotine gum and methadone tablets, as per Lonny's orders.

This was to be his last 911 ride. He was diagnosed with a collapsed left lung, and was admitted to the hospital into intensive care.

After a few days, he was operated on. When it was

over, the doctor told us that the prognosis was not good. He asked if Lonny had a living will, but I was unable to find one. That meant if he was on life support, they could not pull the plug.

His condition worsened. A tube, attached to a ventilator that passed down his trachea, was inserted to help with his breathing. Eventually, another tube went into his nose and down to his stomach for feeding purposes. Two tubes were placed in his right lung which was quickly deteriorating. With all those tubes and equipment, it looked like a downhill battle.

Alan and I, and Greg and Sally would visit him at different times every day. He greeted us with a wide grin with his "joie de vivre" still evident. Despite the circumstances, he remained, or at least tried to remain, his cheerful self. We got permission to bring Lola a few times, and both their faces lit up the room. Speak about joy!

Greg and Lonny were the best of friends and they displayed loving warmth and happiness every time he came to visit. Actually, Greg and Sally were the twosome, but the nurses drew other conclusions.

When they alluded to Greg and Lonny being a couple, Macho Greg and Macho Lonny burst out laughing. It was not much of a burst from Lonny, but it really tickled his wonderful sense of humor.

Marlena wrote Lonny a letter when she learned he was in the hospital. This is an excerpt from that letter of June 10, 2010, that we read to him:

> Dear Lonny!
>
> It's been sooo long since we last talked. That day before the operation I came home about 5 or something but it was too late.... I miss our conversations every day so much, I get used to it, you were like a heroin(?) to me. ☺
>
> It is great that your mother is such a kind person that she tells me how you are. I began taking anti-depressives and it's 14 days now. I feel a little better, but I feel guilty talking to you how I feel, when you must be suffering like I hope that you don't feel pain, that they give you medicine for pain. (I am sorry for my English Lonny)
>
> We have terrible summer here you know. It's

so cold. And it's raining again now (rain every day). I was wondering if nosey woman came to visit you. She misses you also probably. It is time to go to bed now, (you know me) I hope, that this letter will be by your side in few days.

<u>I pray for you Lonny</u>, don't give up, keep the fight, you are so strong!!

Kisses

Marlena

The joy of receiving her letter was reflected in his weak smile. He loved her deeply, and it showed.

At times we would bring Lonny's laptop to the hospital. If he was up to it, he would do catch-up. We helped him send an e-mail to Marlena answering her hopeful and touching letter. He could not spend much time with the laptop because he tired so easily.

The tube that helped his breathing was no longer effective. A tracheotomy tube had to be inserted through his throat. He was unable to talk and had to communicate with a pad and pencil. How frustrating that was for him, and saddened us that much more.

The worst, that was yet to come, arrived. He was moved to a room down the hall, farther away from the nurses' station. That was a sign that there was not much time left. Matt flew in from California to be with us.

We were told by the doctor that his other lung had collapsed, and that there did not seem to be much hope. He was being put in a medically induced coma. They would be feeding him Propofol intravenously, a drug that is administered to terminal patients who are in pain, and who have weeks or days left to live. Michael Jackson died of a self-administered overdose of this drug.

We continued to visit him every day. During our daily visits, we were told that he could be taken off the Propofol for fifteen minutes, and we could communicate with him while he was conscious. As we sat with him, touching hands and sharing our love, Lonny still had hopes of making it through.

During one of these fifteen minute sessions, Lonny told us about an incident that was deeply disturbing.

While he was under sedation, one of the male attendants who was changing the bed linens, was treating him roughly and making fun of him. Oh, if that sick lowlife could have changed places with my sweet-natured Lonny!

We soon realized that the time had come to pull the plug, and for his suffering to end. Watching the tubes being pulled and the equipment being shut down was heartbreaking. He was put on morphine and transferred to the Hospice section of the hospital.

HOSPICE

A patient is put in hospice when medical treatment can no longer cure him. There he is given end-of-life care with comfort and dignity, and morphine for his pain-wracked body. They try to make the person's passing as comfortable as possible. If they wish so, a clergyman is called in to pray and comfort the family and friends.

As we waited around sadly and expectantly, Lonny had other plans. Did he want to hang around because of his family, his friends, his love for living, or was it the morphine? I suspect it was all of the above!

On the list of Lonny's character traits, stubbornness would be near the top. This he displayed by refusing to let go. We were told to speak to him and to tell him that we were ready for him to leave us.

I leaned over his bed and I kissed him. I told him that I loved him, that I would miss him very much, that it hurt me for him to be hurting, and that it was time for him to go. I kissed him again and said goodbye. I sat down in the rocking chair in his room and waited awhile. Then I left.

At three A.M. that morning I received a call from hospice that he had passed. It was finally over. Goodbye my Lonny Love.

The Death Certificate stated the cause of death:

End Stage Chronic Obstructive Pulmonary Disease - C.O.P.D.

A FACEBOOK CHAT

Before Lonny entered the last rehab program, he and Betty were close friends in New York City. They were more than that, they were lovers and drug compatriots and were constantly together. They rode the raptures of mainlining and other more exotic drug adventures. They helped each other through the D.T.'s and other horrors.

Then things changed. After he completed the program, Lonny started attending N.A. meetings again. That is when Lonny met Sally! There was an instant attraction that ended any other amorous attachments that he had.

When Sally moved into her new love's apartment on East Seventy-First Street, it left Betty high and unhappy. She would drop by the apartment, and hang around. Finally, Sally, sensing that this was not a good thing, asked her to leave, and never allowed her back. The relationship was over, but Lonny and Betty were still left with deep feelings for each other.

Betty eventually was able to battle her addiction and recovered. She was a college graduate, very bright, and became a therapist. She moved South where she opened several drug rehab centers, and became very successful specializing in treating addiction. They visited each other on two occasions, and stayed in touch regularly via the internet. She and I became friends on Facebook.

I recently found a Facebook chat that she and I had during Lonny's last days. Can you imagine the sadness I feel writing this?

June 12, 2010

> Gloria: I tried to call you, but I may not have the right number. Lonny is very, very sick in the hospital. They almost pulled the plug on Thursday, but we did not allow it. His lungs shut down, and he is on a respirator in a drug-induced coma. So far there is a slight improvement. It's one day at a

time. We are praying. I know he would want you to know. I'll keep in touch.

June 17, 2010

Gloria: It was a tough day today. He was awake for awhile, but it was frustrating for him and for us. He wanted to talk so badly but with the tube in his mouth he couldn't. We tried different ways of communicating but they didn't work. They tried weaning him from the ventilator but that didn't work either. Hoping tomorrow will be better.

June 18, 2010

Betty: I understand the frustration. My brother had the breathing tube in his mouth after liver transplant surgery. We communicated with paper and pencil. Thank you for the update. My wish for today is for Lonny to have some peace. Tell him that I love him and will come to see him as soon as he is able to see me. Would you please let me know when I can come. Thank you. Take care of yourself, Mrs. Lichtenberg and stay strong.....still in my prayers. XXOO to Lon

June 19, 2010

Gloria: We tried the writing, but it didn't work. Things are pretty much the same. They will try again to wean him today. Will let you know later.

June 20, 2010

Gloria: Today was good. The nurse reduced his sedative, so he was awake and aware for a few hours. Of course, he can't talk, but he responds by shaking his head. We held hands most of the time. Alan has been with me all along, and there was so much love among us. He had a great nurse. I don't know if tomorrow's nurse will be so accommodating. His face looks so beautiful. Let's keep praying.

June 24, 2010

Gloria: Sorry my computer had a virus. It's now fixed. Lonny had a tracheotomy today. We're hoping it will ease his breathing a little. Things don't really look too good. I'm sorry and very sad.

June 28, 2010

> Gloria: Things are very bad. Prepare yourself. I'll let you know.

July 2, 2010

> Gloria: Lonny died this morning, 7/2/10. I know how you felt about each other.

July 3, 2010

> Betty: I am so sorry. When is the funeral? I was completely immobilized yesterday, bedridden as a matter of fact.

July 3, 2010

> Gloria: It was a real trial by ordeal. He was so lucid two days before he died, but he couldn't talk because of the trach, and we were all so frustrated. Believe it or not, we were laughing and it was the old Lonny. In hospice, they were feeding him drugs to help with the pain, and he wouldn't let go. My sweet, darling Lonny. He was the best. The funeral is Monday, here in Boynton Beach at 10:15.

September 6, 2012

> Betty: I love this picture. My Lonikins is smiling, so sweet. I have not been well. I have breast cancer stage IV. Now for the good news, I am now friends with Greg, he's a nice guy. Well Gloria, hope life is treating you kindly, you are a wonderful woman. Keep the faith and Peace.

September 11, 2012

> Gloria: So glad to hear from you, but so sorry to hear your news. I miss my Lonny so much. We were so close in every way. Everything reminds me of him - shopping in the supermarket, T.V. shows we shared, sooo much. Just was in touch with Greg. He's doing better, but will always miss his Sally and his Lonny. Lola, Lonny's dog, lives right near him, and she's doing well with her new owner. Feel better, and keep in touch. I'll pray for you.

END OF FACEBOOK CHAT.

I found this Facebook chat with Betty after I wrote the previous chapter. Betty died shortly after of cancer.

THE FUNERAL

In 2008, two years before he died, Lonny made an unusual request. He asked me to purchase a cemetery plot for him in the same cemetery that my husband was buried, and where I would lie as well. It so happened that we were able to buy a resale, a double plot, which was a few steps away from ours. He would share this plot with Alan.

That taken care of, we made arrangements at the chapel for his someday funeral. Lonny took pleasure in choosing a tasteful and costly casket. He still enjoyed the better things in life, in this case, in death, too. Everything was ready for what was to be inevitable, but untimely, in 2010.

Shortly before the day of the funeral, the Rabbi met with us to get background on Lonny. We looked at each other because we did not think it was fitting to tell him that his greatest accomplishments were as a drug dealer, a recycling clerk, a survivor of Riker's Island, or a grower of marijuana. However, we were able to truly say that he was a loving son and brother, a faithful and giving friend, and a devoted Lola lover. He was a liberal thinker and cared for the plight of the poor and the unfortunate. He was interested in politics and a devotee of sports, especially Mixed Martial Arts. Though he had his trials and tribulations, he enjoyed the good times in his life, and he wanted those around him to be happy, too. He was a Mensch!

We did not give the Rabbi much to work with, but he was inspired with our display of deep loss and love for Lonny.

It was the day of the funeral, and the chapel filled. Though it was July, the quiet season in Florida, most of the seats were taken. It could be said that it was a Standing Room Only (SRO) performance for this once Actor's Equity member in his final appearance.

The service began. The Rabbi gave a touching eulogy for Lonny that evoked sadness and tears.

Matt spoke next.

MATT'S EULOGY

One of Lon's biggest joys in life was the Buy One Get One Free sale at the super- market. Not because he got two for the price of one, because some people say that they jack up the price before putting it on sale, but so that he could have one for himself and the other to give to my mom, a friend, or a neighbor who just happened to drop by that day.

When we sat down with the Rabbi to try and explain who Lonny was, we didn't have the typical My Son the Jewish Doctor story. There was no great academic achievement, no great career or financial success story to tell. And in truth, the things we had to say about who Lonny was are the only things that matter when the time comes to meet your maker. Lonny was our younger brother and grew up in the shadows of a lawyer and accountant.

But everyone is different and Lon chose a different path. There is no doubt in my mind that he would have been a superstar in any field he chose to pursue. He would have been a better accountant than I, a better lawyer than Alan, or the head writer for Seinfeld, if that's what he chose to do.

If you got to know Lon at all, for just a few minutes, you knew he was someone special. And if you were lucky enough to get to know him well, you had no choice but to fall uncontrollably in love. I don't know anyone kinder or more compassionate than Lon. He oozed it out of every pore of his body.

He was the funniest person I know, and it would be impossible for me to count the number of times we laughed until we cried. Nobody made me laugh as much, and I'm sure nobody will.

Faced with the overwhelming obstacles he had, only Lonny knew the true magnitude. He was always the first to give and the last to take. George Eliot said, "What do we live for, if it is not to make life less difficult for each other?" That was Lonny, always thinking of himself last.

We're beyond grateful for the years we had, but it kills me that my young children will grow up not knowing the kindness, compassion, and love of Lon. Our family will never be the same, but in our solace, we thank God, not for the length, but the quality of time we had with him, and that he is now in peace. Lonny truly enjoyed life, and we take comfort in knowing he was surrounded by the people who loved and cared for him as much as they did for themselves.

If the next fifty years pass as quickly as the first, I'll see you very soon my brother. We love you more than can possibly be expressed in words, and fortunately, you knew that. Lonny, rest in peace.

Matt and Lonny -
Mutual respect, admiration and love.

THE BURIAL

When the services were over, a few announcements were made and instructions were given. Everyone was invited back to my house after the interment.

The casket was carried out, and we followed the hearse to the cemetery. When we arrived, we were directed to a canopy that was set up near the grave. The Rabbi recited the prayers and the casket was lowered into the ground. We, the mourners, were given a shovel with earth to cast over the casket. It symbolized a final act of love and kindness for the deceased, our beloved Lonny.

We sadly returned to my house where a light repast had been set up by my friends. Shiva, the period of mourning, had begun and lasted for four days in my home. My dear friends came to comfort us through this time.

This over, another difficult, dreaded task awaited us.

CLEAN-UP TIME

Settling the affairs, putting things in order and cleaning up are probably the most difficult things to deal with after the death of a loved one.

Lonny's financial holdings were no problem, as there were none. We advised the different services he had of his demise and sent Death Certificates as needed. His breathing equipment and other paraphernalia had to be returned.

Alan decided he would move to Florida and live in the condo, with Matt's approval. The apartment had to be ready for his takeover, so we started the clean-up. There really wasn't that much to do because Alan would be staying there.

I went through his night tables. Among many other

things, I found white socks, medication, condoms, vaginal jelly, nicotine gum and cough drops. His friend Greg recently told me that Lonny, until his last trip to the hospital, was sexually active with a local young lady that he met on the internet. No surprise, considering his physical equipment.

There were still remnants of the lighting from his marijuana project. They were a memento of his tremendous success as a pot grower.

We found adult videos piled in his closet and had to decide on the best way to dispose of them. We dropped them in a dumpster in the dark of night.

Lonny had a large supply of C.O.P.D. medication that we donated to a free health clinic, for which they were very grateful.

We gave his cabinetful of BOGO coffee to a local soup kitchen.

I took Lonny's plants, some of which are still alive.

I could not deal with disposing of his clothing, so I left them for a future time.

Lola was the most difficult of all. Though I love dogs, I was not physically able to care for her. We lucked out because Greg and Sally had a neighbor, Shirley, who had two other dogs. She happily added Lola to her dog family. Lola loved to ride in a car, and Shirley would take her on her daily business stops. They lived near the beach, a perfect setting for Lola. It would have made Lonny happy to see her so comfortably placed.

The rest of his furnishings remained in place, his TV's, the paintings on the wall, his beautiful rug, and his tasteful knickknacks. When I visit Alan, most everything is a reminder of Lonny.

CONDOLENCES

As is customary, we received many condolences, some as contributions to The American Lung Association, The Pap Corps, our local cancer group, Trees for Israel and other charities.

The following is a card we received from Marlena, his Albanian love:

> "Dear mother of Lonny!
>
> My sincerest condolences. I will be with you with prayers!
>
> I would just like to say, that Lonny really loved you. All of you.
>
> We were talking every day for hours. I can explain how I feel sad.

He will be mine forever.

Marlena"

Marlena had lost her Lonny and could no longer look forward to coming to the United States to be with him.

THE UNVEILING

It is Jewish tradition to hold a service when the gravestone is viewed for the first time. This usually takes place before the first anniversary of the person's death. It is called an unveiling.

Alan, Matt and I planned our own services. We invited Greg, Sally and a few others.

Greg and Sally were Lonny's dearest and closest friends. They saw each other every day and shared their joys, sorrows and problems. They were with him in the hospital daily, and in the Hospice when he died. It is not usual, but I thought it fitting, to honor them on the gravestone. Lonny would have happily approved.

We prepared a script that we followed.

"Our beloved Lonny died on July 2, 2010. Today we gather to remember him and to dedicate a monument in his memory."

We read Psalms 8, 121 and 23, and said the prayers. We each shared our feelings, and I read my "Who Is Lonny?" poem, but I changed it to "Who Was Lonny?"

Before the concluding prayer, the memorial was consecrated and unveiled.

LON IAN LICHTENBERG

1961 - 2010

BELOVED SON

BROTHER AND FRIEND

Rest in peace, Lonny. All we have left of you are our memories.

Lonny Love, you are missed!

THE MEMORIES

More than four years have passed since Lonny died, and my thoughts of him have hardly diminished. Not a day goes by that I do not think of him.

Reminders of him are ever present. Let me count the ways:

1. Pictures of Lonny - There is a photo of him over my sink, in my office and on my bedroom wall. The New York Times Sunday Guide, with him as Randy the Clown in "Broken Toys" on the cover, is on my foyer wall;

2. Dogs – Whenever I see dogs on T.V. or being walked, especially a Maltese;

3. T.V. – The programs we watched together,

specials about Aids, series about drugs and drug addicts (Breaking Bad was a long one), cigarette and nicotine gum commercials, Howard Stern on America's Got Talent, and many more;

4. Facebook – I still visit his page;

5. The supermarket – The BOGO's, the sections where I shopped for him for coffee, cereal, produce, bakery and deli;

6. Plants – I still have the ficus tree he gave me for my birthday, and the plants I rescued from his house;

7. Politics – He was overjoyed when President Obama was elected in 2008; He would not be overjoyed with the politics and happenings in the news these days;

8. Marijuana in the news – He would have been elated with the progress of the legalization of pot. If he were alive, the day might have come that he could grow his wonderful crop of marijuana in his walk-in closet again, for medical reasons, of course;

9. Dreams – I sometimes dream about him.

Though he had his trials and tribulations, like Voltaire's Candide, Lonny still believed it is the best of all possible worlds, and that is how he tried to live it.

It did not take much to make him laugh, giggle or smile. Lonny still found happiness wherever and whenever he could. He had an indomitable nature and he never gave up on life. Life gave up on him.

Those of us who loved him are grateful for his having added laughter, now turned to smiles, to our lives. We are thankful for Lonny Love's having been!

ACKNOWLEDGEMENT AND THANK YOU

1. Thank you Alan Lichtenberg for being at my side whenever I needed you, for filling me in with your recollections, for making me an expert in photo resizing and cropping, and so much more. I could not have done it without you.

2. Thank you Matt Lichtenberg for taking the time to fly in from California to give me your input and help me flesh out the story, for your tender and loving memories of Lonny that you displayed so beautifully in your eulogy.

3. Thank you to my dearest friend, Gerald Lieberman, who was always available as a sounding board and advisor, and ready to help me in this publishing process that was so new to me, and that at times I found very difficult. That's what friends are for!

4. Thank you Seth Taylor for your important contributions to the writing of this book.

5. Thank you Barbara and Rick Foster and their beautiful Bella.

6. Thanks to my overflowing "Lonny File", in which I have over the years accumulated letters, bills, documents, reports, photographs, tapes, etc., for making it possible for me to write this story.

ABOUT THE AUTHOR

Gloria Lichtenberg was born in the Bronx, N.Y. where she and her husband, Frank, raised their sons Alan, Matthew and Lonny. During her career as a sixth grade teacher she wrote songs that she used for teaching in her classroom. Some of her past students still remember her Grammar Songs.

Due to the circumstances she described in the book, she had to leave New York City, or her health would suffer. She and her husband retired and settled in Boynton Beach, Florida. Not long after moving into her new condo, she set up a Drama Club. She helped in the production of musicals for which she co-wrote the lyrics, and assisted in the directing.

She wrote "Children's Know-It-All Songs," a book of original songs for Early Childhood teachers. She has happily given her music books as gifts to be used in the classrooms here and as far away as Kenya.

She credits Facebook for affording her the joy of being in contact with many of her past students, and bringing back fond memories.

www.ingramcontent.com/pod-product-compliance
Lightning Source LLC
Chambersburg PA
CBHW051940160426
43198CB00013B/2240